Quiet Time for the Expecta

Develop great faith as your little one

Copyright@2019 JournalsByCatherine aka Cathy Idowu
Published in the USA.
First Edition April 30th, 2019

ISBN 978-0-9801484-6-6

Cover and interior design, weekly reflections, and daily scripture selection by Cathy Idowu

Published by Ritequest Publishing

For contact and permissions:

Cathy Idowu
journalsbycatherine@gmail.com
Ritequest Publishing
Florida, USA

Dear *Expectant mother*, congratulations on your big news and blessings to you and your growing baby! This prayer journal has been designed to help you come confidently before God in prayer and gratitude, enjoying the benefit of quiet time as you prepare for the arrival of your precious little one. God said to the prophet, Jeremiah: Before you were in your mother's womb, I knew you. It can be hard to imagine that your unseen baby is so well known to God. That is the premise of this journal. The daily scriptures bring both you and your baby before the Lord. The reflections contained are designed to help launch you into praying, not just while your baby is in your womb, but also for the future: God's purpose for him or her. Furthermore, both scriptures and reflections serve up faith-building verses to prepare you for joyful challenges of motherhood.

Record your notable experiences along the way, and hopefully, this will be a beautiful keepsake with treasured memories you can, one day in the future, share with your child. God always wants us to keep a record of His faithfulness to us, and this journal provides you with an opportunity to fulfill that.

Contents and use of this journal

◆ A page to record the excitement of your baby's gender reveal moment and celebration. It also includes a photo spot for the ultrasound evidence!

◆ A page to journal the process of choosing your baby's or babies' (if multiples) name(s).

◆ Two pages to record notable things and God-moments

◆ Two pages to keep a record of kindness shown you by family, friends, and those people God brought alongside you to share this special season.

◆ A "security blanket" coloring page to color and pen down 12 promises you're praying over your baby.

◆ The daily journal section is divided into 12 weeks. Each week starts with a faith-building devotion, encouraging reflection and prayer. Have a Bible handy to read the assigned passage so that you might follow the insight presented. The journal pages for the next 5 days include daily scriptures and sections to record what God is speaking to your heart— that is the "Word for my soul" section. Next, is a space for gratitude followed by your prayer requests. Finally, you'll have an opportunity to cast off that besetting anxiety that may be overwhelming you during this period. (You may find that you are continually casting that same anxiety day after day. Keep at it. God cares for you and desires you to strengthen your faith in Him, setting you free from your anxiety). For the weekend, you have a blank notes page—your anything catch-all page. Include your ideas, thoughts, to-dos, etc. In total, you have three months or a complete trimester worth of journaling pages.

God's blessings upon the fruit of your womb! (Deuteronomy 28: 4)

Cathy Idowu

This journal belongs to:

_____

Positively pregnant! Date: _____

Mother   Father

_____ _____

"For this child I prayed"

1 Samuel 1:27

Boy? or Girl?

The day we found out _____

How we shared our story with the world...

Baby name:

Origin:

Meaning:

Why this name?

Baby name:

Origin:

Meaning:

Why this name?

Baby name:

Origin:

Meaning:

Why this name?

She treasured these things in her heart...

Luke 2:19

Quotes & happenings to treasure...

...Whatever things are true, whatever things are honorable, whatever things are just, whatever things are pure, whatever things are lovely, whatever things are of good report; if there is any virtue, and if there is any praise, think about these things.

Philippians 4:8

Remembering to give thanks for friendships, gifts, encouragement, support, and random acts of kindness...

Bless the Lord,
O my soul,
and forget
none of His
benefits...

Psalm 103:2

This is Week # _____ Date _____
_____
_____
_____
_____
_____
_____
_____
_____
_____

Conceiving with purpose

Read the reference passage: 1 Samuel 1:1-20

Reference Verse: In her deep anguish Hannah prayed to the LORD, weeping bitterly. 11 And she made a vow, saying, "LORD Almighty, if you will only look on your servant's misery and remember me, and not forget your servant but give her a son, then I will give him to the LORD for all the days of his life..." 1 Samuel 1:10

Insight

Difficulty churns away at our motives allowing the cream to rise to the top. See how Hannah's motives became purified over time, allowing God to receive the best from her as she learned to persevere through her struggles and deep desires. Her prayers might have been initially self-focused, and fixed upon finding a way to heal from the hurts of Peninnah's scoffing. Over time, her vision expanded to include prayers for a higher purpose: It was no longer about Peninnah, no longer about herself, but about God's glory.

Reflection: Hannah had a specific prayer request for the child she desired. Her prayers for her hoped-for son had a long view in mind that included "all the days of his life." Reflect on the prayers you are praying for your little one. It's never too early to start praying purpose-driven prayers.

For meditation: The insistent prayer of a righteous person is powerfully effective. James 5:16

Date:

Your hands have made me and formed me. Give me understanding, that I may learn your commandments.

Psalm 119:73

Today's word for my soul...

I'm thankful for...

Prayer focus and requests...

Casting this care upon the Lord...

Date:

Your eyes saw me when I was formless;
all my days were written in Your book and planned
before a single one of them began.

Psalm 139:16 (HCSB)

Today's word for my soul...

I'm thankful for...

Prayer focus and requests...

Casting this care upon the Lord...

In nothing be anxious, but in everything, by prayer and petition with thanksgiving, let your requests be made known to God. And the peace of God, which surpasses all understanding, will guard your hearts and your thoughts in Christ Jesus. Philippians 4:6-7

Today's word for my soul...

I'm thankful for...

Prayer focus and requests...

Casting this care upon the Lord...

Date:

You will keep whoever's mind is steadfast in
perfect peace, because he trusts in you.

Isaiah 26:3

Today's word for my soul...

I'm thankful for...

Prayer focus and requests...

Casting this care upon the Lord...

Date:

I will instruct you and teach you in the way which you shall go. I will counsel you with my eye on you.

Psalm 32:8

Today's word for my soul...

I'm thankful for...

Prayer focus and requests...

Casting this care upon the Lord...

Weekly notes...

This is Week#   Date _____

_____

_____

_____

_____

_____

_____

_____

_____

Sign-up for unconventional worship

Read the reference passage: Luke 7:36-50

Reference Verse: Standing behind at his feet weeping, she began to wet his feet with her tears, and she wiped them with the hair of her head, kissed his feet, and anointed them with the ointment. Luke 7:38

Insight

Wouldn't you consider this type of worship unconventional? There is no record of this being the standard for worship, but out of the overflow of a grateful heart that this woman had toward Jesus, she pulled whatever resources she had and worshipped. Pregnancy might mean some of the predictable practices you've come to rely on for worship become subdued. It may be morning sickness, or hormones causing your mind or body to feel a little different, or even a prescribed bed rest, forcing you to forgo your usual active Sunday praise and worship. Rather than get frustrated, get creative. This woman teaches us that where there's a will to worship, you'll come up with a way. The psalmist even said, "let the faithful sing with joy in their beds…" (Psalm 149:5). By any means necessary, make a way to keep your grateful heart of worship going.

Reflection: Think about the conventional ways you've always shown your gratitude to God by serving, or worshipping. Has any of that been challenged during this special season of pregnancy? What have you learned from this woman about the mindset to overcome those limitations or barriers? How did Jesus react to her efforts?

For meditation: Shout triumphantly to the Lord, all the earth. Serve the Lord with gladness; come before Him with joyful song. Psalm 11:1-2 (HCSB)

He will feed his flock like a shepherd. He will gather the lambs in his arm, and carry them in his bosom. He will gently lead those who have their young.

Isaiah 40:11

Today's word for my soul...

I'm thankful for...

Prayer focus and requests...

Casting this care upon the Lord...

Date:

See how great a love the Father has given to us, that we should be called children of God!

1 John 3:1

Today's word for my soul...

_____
_____
_____
_____
_____
_____
_____
_____

I'm thankful for...

_____
_____
_____
_____

Prayer focus and requests...

_____
_____
_____
_____
_____
_____

Casting this care upon the Lord...

_____
_____
_____

Date:

He restores my soul. He guides me in the paths of righteousness for his name's sake.

Psalm 23:3

Today's word for my soul...

_____
_____
_____
_____
_____
_____
_____
_____
_____

I'm thankful for...

_____
_____
_____
_____

Prayer focus and requests...

_____
_____
_____
_____
_____
_____

Casting this care upon the Lord...

_____
_____
_____

Date:

The eternal God is your dwelling place. Underneath are the everlasting arms.

Deuteronomy 33:27

Today's word for my soul...

_____
_____
_____
_____
_____
_____
_____

I'm thankful for...

_____
_____
_____
_____

Prayer focus and requests...

_____
_____
_____
_____
_____

Casting this care upon the Lord...

_____
_____
_____

Date:

Praise the LORD, my soul; all my inmost being, praise his holy name. Praise the LORD, my soul, and forget not all his benefits—
Psalm 103:1-2 (NIV)

Today's word for my soul...

I'm thankful for...

Prayer focus and requests...

Casting this care upon the Lord...

Weekly notes...

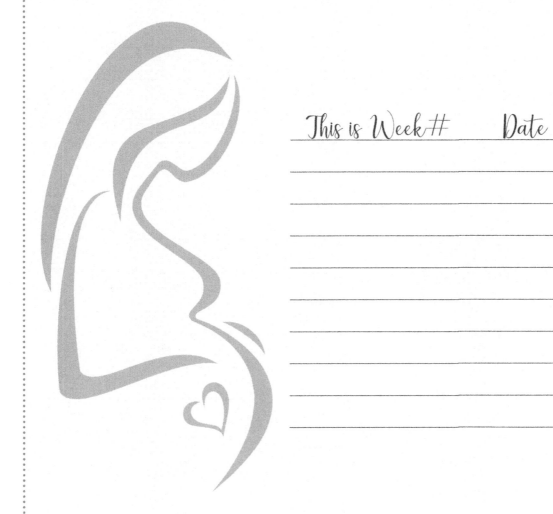

This is Week #   Date

_____

_____

_____

_____

_____

_____

_____

_____

_____

Even hormones submit to Him

Read the reference passage: Luke 8:43-48

Reference Verse: He said to her, "Daughter, cheer up. Your faith has made you well. Go in peace." Luke 8:48

Insight

Plagued with hormone issues, countless medicine bottles, constant transfers from one physician to another, and 12 years later, this woman still found no healing. Then the great physician passed by. She was not holding back, pressing through the crowd, filled with trust and desperation, she touched the hem of His garment. This was her prayer. It was embarrassing and would remain unspoken. She had reached out to him quietly and discreetly, hoping for a hushed-up miracle. But to the Lord, it was not quiet. This was a big deal. Someone was reaching out to Him in faith. Jesus' ability to heal is not an impersonal force, but instead, it is intensely personal to Him. It is a compassionate tug at His heart as power is released with love. Then Jesus called on her. Not to embarrass her, but to share her testimony. He was inviting her to hold her head up high, forget her shame, and encourage other women.

Reflection: Pregnancy comes with a boat-load of hormonal activity, and some manifest in ways that may be unpleasant. Others are issues that remain unspoken beyond the doctor's office, year after year. Would you give up on seeking help, especially after 12 years of no success? Did this woman write herself off as hopeless? Are you encouraged to press into Jesus, by faith? What did Jesus say to this woman? Expect that He will say the same to you.

For meditation: Let us therefore draw near with boldness to the throne of grace, that we may receive mercy, and may find grace for help in time of need. Hebrews 4:16

Yes, you have been with me from birth; from my mother's womb you have cared for me. No wonder I am always praising you!

Psalm 71:6 (NLT)

Today's word for my soul...

_____
_____
_____
_____
_____
_____
_____
_____
_____

I'm thankful for...

_____
_____
_____
_____

Prayer focus and requests...

_____
_____
_____
_____
_____
_____

Casting this care upon the Lord...

_____
_____
_____

Date:

All your children will be taught by the LORD, and great will be their peace.

Isaiah 54:13 (NIV)

Today's word for my soul...

_____
_____
_____
_____
_____
_____
_____

I'm thankful for...

_____
_____
_____
_____

Prayer focus and requests...

_____
_____
_____
_____
_____

Casting this care upon the Lord...

_____
_____
_____

Date:

LORD, You have searched me and known me.
You know when I sit down and when I stand up;
You understand my thoughts from far away.

Psalm 139:1-2 (HCSB)

Today's word for my soul...

I'm thankful for...

Prayer focus and requests...

Casting this care upon the Lord...

Date:

You search out my path and my lying down, and are acquainted with all my ways.

Psalm 139:3

Today's word for my soul...

_____
_____
_____
_____
_____
_____
_____
_____
_____

I'm thankful for...

_____
_____
_____
_____
_____

Prayer focus and requests...

_____
_____
_____
_____
_____
_____

Casting this care upon the Lord...

_____
_____
_____

You Yourself have recorded my wanderings. Put my tears in Your bottle. Are they not in Your records?

Psalm 56:8 (HCSB)

Today's word for my soul...

_____
_____
_____
_____
_____
_____
_____
_____
_____

I'm thankful for...

_____
_____
_____
_____

Prayer focus and requests...

_____
_____
_____
_____
_____
_____

Casting this care upon the Lord...

_____
_____
_____

Weekly notes...

This is Week #   Date
_____
_____
_____
_____
_____
_____
_____
_____
_____

The mindset needed for godly expansion

Read the reference passage: Numbers 13:16-14:9

Reference Verse: The land we passed through and explored is exceedingly good. If the Lord is pleased with us, he will lead us into that land, a land flowing with milk and honey, and will give it to us. Numbers 14:7-8 (NIV)

Insight

An expansion is upon you, as evidenced by your growing baby in your womb. Your family is expanding. This is of great delight in the sight of the Lord who commanded us with a blessing to go forth and multiply, in order to fill and replenish the earth. He gave this command along with a blessing that you would be able to accomplish it. But how about the mindset? Is your mind keeping in step with the high expectation of this expansion? The account in the reference passage shows that though the Lord has gifted us with the ability to expand, it is possible to still have a mindset of timidity. With all that God had done to favor them, 10 of their 12 spies assessed themselves as feeble grasshoppers. This mindset cannot accomplish the great things that God has planned for you. Joshua and Caleb, however, had the right mindset. Instead of assessing their ability, they put their confidence in God, saying: If the Lord were pleased with them, they would inherit the land.

Reflection: When you consider the things needed for this delightful expansion of your family, are you overwhelmed? Are you anxious about your inability to possess all that God has for you? Or are you filled with the confident faith of Joshua and Caleb?

For meditation: Without faith it is impossible to be well pleasing to him, for he who comes to God must believe that he exists, and that he is a rewarder of those who seek him. Hebrews 11:6

Date:

Children are a gift from the LORD; they are a reward from him.

Psalm 127:3 (NLT)

Today's word for my soul...

_____
_____
_____
_____
_____
_____
_____
_____

I'm thankful for...

_____
_____
_____

Prayer focus and requests...

_____
_____
_____
_____
_____
_____

Casting this care upon the Lord...

_____
_____
_____

Date:

Then God blessed them and said, "Be fruitful and multiply.
Fill the earth and govern it.
Genesis 1:28 (NLT)

Today's word for my soul...

I'm thankful for...

Prayer focus and requests...

Casting this care upon the Lord...

I lift up my eyes to the mountains—where does my help come from? My help comes from the Lord, the Maker of heaven and earth.

Psalm 121:1-2 (NIV)

Today's word for my soul...

I'm thankful for...

Prayer focus and requests...

Casting this care upon the Lord...

Date:

For we are his workmanship, created in Christ Jesus for good works, which God prepared before that we would walk in them. Ephesians 2:10

Today's word for my soul...

_____
_____
_____
_____
_____
_____
_____
_____

I'm thankful for...

_____
_____
_____
_____

Prayer focus and requests...

_____
_____
_____
_____
_____
_____

Casting this care upon the Lord...

_____
_____
_____

I tell you, keep asking, and it will be given you. Keep seeking, and you will find. Keep knocking, and it will be opened to you. For everyone who asks receives. He who seeks finds. To him who knocks it will be opened.　　Luke 11:9-10

Today's word for my soul...

I'm thankful for...

Prayer focus and requests...

Casting this care upon the Lord...

Weekly notes...

This is Week# _____ Date _____

_____

_____

_____

_____

_____

_____

_____

_____

Great joy will overcome great discomfort

Read the reference passage: Luke 2:1-20

Reference Verse: The angel said to them, "Don't be afraid, for behold, I bring you good news of great joy which will be to all the people. For there is born to you today, in David's city, a Savior, who is Christ the Lord." Luke 2:10-11

Insight

We can't avoid those less than perfect circumstances that come our way from time to time. But what of when it's "unfortunately" ill-timed with a special occasion, such as the birth of a child? Now think of Mary. She was to birth Jesus, the Savior of the world. In her humanity, it's hard to imagine she wouldn't have expected the angels to roll out the red carpet for her: *Shut down the inn, supply the coziest room and bed, have doting midwives attending. After all, a VIP was being born. The Savior of the world!* Did God forget? Of course not. If anything, in the midst of the manure, He confirmed it through the angelic declaration. "I bring you good news of great joy...for there is born to you, a Savior who is Christ the Lord." There was not one mention of the imperfect setting—just joy heralded. This is the heart of Jesus— to endure a present challenge for the sake of future joy.

Reflection: As you await your baby, what is your imperfect circumstance? Maybe you're away from loved ones and lonely. Perhaps there is a loss of needed income, health limitations, or the understandable weariness of life. You fill in your blanks. Now think of heaven's perspective. What would God like you to prioritize: momentary discomfort or the great joy to follow?

For meditation: Let this mind be in you that was also in Christ Jesus. Philippians 2:5(KJV)

They will not labor in vain, nor will they bear children doomed to misfortune; for they will be a people blessed by the Lord, they and their descendants with them.

Isaiah 65:23 (NIV)

Today's word for my soul...

_____
_____
_____
_____
_____
_____
_____
_____
_____
_____

I'm thankful for...

_____
_____
_____
_____

Prayer focus and requests...

_____
_____
_____
_____
_____
_____

Casting this care upon the Lord...

_____
_____
_____

Date:

I will pour my Spirit on your descendants, and my blessing on your offspring.

Isaiah 44:3

Today's word for my soul...

I'm thankful for...

Prayer focus and requests...

Casting this care upon the Lord...

What eye did not see and ear did not hear, and what never entered the human mind—God prepared this for those who love Him.   1 Corinthians 2:9 (HCSB)

Today's word for my soul...

I'm thankful for...

Prayer focus and requests...

Casting this care upon the Lord...

Date:

Blessed be the God and Father of our Lord Jesus Christ, who has blessed us with every spiritual blessing in the heavenly places in Christ.

Ephesians 1:3

Today's word for my soul...

_____
_____
_____
_____
_____
_____
_____
_____

I'm thankful for...

_____
_____
_____
_____

Prayer focus and requests...

_____
_____
_____
_____
_____

Casting this care upon the Lord...

_____
_____
_____

His divine power has given us everything required for life
and godliness through the knowledge of Him who called us
by His own glory and goodness.

1 Peter 2:3 (HCSB)

Today's word for my soul...

I'm thankful for...

Prayer focus and requests...

Casting this care upon the Lord...

Weekly notes...

This is Week #   Date

_____

_____

_____

_____

_____

_____

_____

_____

_____

Stand still and see His salvation

Read the reference passage: Exodus 2:1-10

Reference Verse: When she could no longer hide him, she took a papyrus basket for him, and coated it with tar and with pitch. She put the child in it, and laid it in the reeds by the river's bank. His sister stood far off, to see what would be done to him.
Exodus 2:3-4

Insight

Here is a woman whose situation was indeed a basket case. National policy deemed her son unfit to live. Wrong DNA, he must die. That was the executive prescription for all Hebrew males born during this period. She was powerless to do anything about it, and so was everyone else in her network of family and friends. A slave woman and a basket weaver, her existence practically worthless to the world around her. But she looked at her son and saw his worth. She would fight for him! Even if that meant doing the only thing within her power to do: laying him in a protective basket she had woven. Her hands laid him at the bank of the Nile, but her heart of faith laid him at God's mercy seat. Fear of the passing crocodiles gave way to faith in the God of her salvation. That faith would later lead to deliverance for all of Israel.

Reflection: There was not much lower one could go—a basket weaving slave woman—but she would become the mother of Israel's great deliverer and giver of the law. All because she acted in faith on behalf of her beloved child. When we're standing silently still and watching, is it because we're resigned in fear of impending trouble, or because we're meditating on God's goodness and awaiting His salvation?

For meditation: My soul, wait in silence for God alone, for my expectation is from him. Psalm 62:5

I will pour my Spirit on your descendants, and my blessing on your offspring.

Isaiah 44:3 (WEB)

Today's word for my soul...

I'm thankful for...

Prayer focus and requests...

Casting this care upon the Lord...

Date:

Hallelujah! Happy is the man who fears the LORD, taking great delight in His commands. His descendants will be powerful in the land; the generation of the upright will be blessed.   Psalm 112:1-2 (HCSB)

Today's word for my soul...

I'm thankful for...

Prayer focus and requests...

Casting this care upon the Lord...

Date:

Search me, God, and know my heart; test me and know my concerns. See if there is any offensive way in me; lead me in the everlasting way.

Psalm 139:23-24 (HCSB)

Today's word for my soul...

_____
_____
_____
_____
_____
_____
_____
_____

I'm thankful for...

_____
_____
_____
_____

Prayer focus and requests...

_____
_____
_____
_____
_____
_____

Casting this care upon the Lord...

_____
_____
_____

Like arrows in the hands of a warrior are children born in one's youth.

Psalm 127:4 (NIV)

Today's word for my soul...

_____
_____
_____
_____
_____
_____
_____

I'm thankful for...

_____
_____
_____
_____

Prayer focus and requests...

_____
_____
_____
_____
_____

Casting this care upon the Lord...

_____
_____
_____

Date:

But the very hairs of your head are all numbered. Therefore
don't be afraid. You are of more value than many sparrows.

Luke 12:7

Today's word for my soul...

I'm thankful for...

Prayer focus and requests...

Casting this care upon the Lord...

Weekly notes...

This is Week #   Date

_____

_____

_____

_____

_____

_____

_____

_____

_____

_____

Planning for an honorable heritage

Read the reference passage: Ruth 1- 4:22

Reference Verse: But Ruth replied, "Don't urge me to leave you or to turn back from you. Where you go I will go, and where you stay I will stay. Your people will be my people and your God my God. Ruth 1:16 (NIV).

Insight

Looking at Naomi, her life was an illustration of everything a woman would dread: lost her husband, lost her sons, lost her worldly possessions. No one would have bet on this old widow. Though it seemed she had nothing, she had the mark of God upon her heritage. Ruth, the Moabite, her daughter-in-law, saw the opportunity to be linked with this blessed heritage and latched on, refusing to let go. The thought of becoming a covenant daughter of Israel meant so much more to her and her future generations than returning to Moab for a supposed better life. If she continued to Bethlehem, there would be hope that her future children would be connected to God, and that was the amazing heritage she sought after.

Reflection: Think about the mindset Ruth had and how she acted on it. Orpah, on the other hand, had a show of emotion but was not passionate enough to follow through on the future hope of being part of God's family. Think about what heritage you would want your child associated with. Do you have the passion it takes to seek it out actively? How did God reward Ruth?

For meditation: But as many as received him, to them he gave the right to become God's children, to those who believe in his name. John 1:12

Date:

From the lips of babes and infants you have established strength.
Psalm 8:2

Today's word for my soul...

I'm thankful for...

Prayer focus and requests...

Casting this care upon the Lord...

Date:

For you are a chosen people…God's very own possession. As a result, you can show others the goodness of God, for he called you out of the darkness into his wonderful light.

1 Peter 2:9 (NLT)

Today's word for my soul…

I'm thankful for…

Prayer focus and requests…

Casting this care upon the Lord…

Oh how great is your goodness, which you have laid
up for those who fear you, which you have worked for
those who take refuge in you, before the sons of men!

Psalm 31:19

Today's word for my soul...

_____
_____
_____
_____
_____
_____
_____
_____
_____
_____

I'm thankful for...

_____
_____
_____
_____

Prayer focus and requests...

_____
_____
_____
_____
_____
_____

Casting this care upon the Lord...

_____
_____
_____
_____

Date:

But those who trust in the Lord will find new strength.
They will soar high on wings like eagles. They will run and
not grow weary. They will walk and not faint.

Isaiah 40:31 (NLT)

Today's word for my soul...

I'm thankful for...

Prayer focus and requests...

Casting this care upon the Lord...

Date:

In everything give thanks, for this is the will of God in
Christ Jesus toward you.

1 Thessalonians 5:18

Today's word for my soul...

I'm thankful for...

Prayer focus and requests...

Casting this care upon the Lord...

Weekly notes...

This is Week #   Date
_____
_____
_____
_____
_____
_____
_____
_____
_____

God's presence is your child's joy

Read the reference passage: Luke 1:39-45

Reference Verse: As soon as the sound of your greeting reached my ears, the baby in my womb leaped for joy... Luke 1:44 (NIV)

Insight

In God's presence, there is fullness of joy (Psalm 16:11), that is an observation the Psalmist made about the effect of God's presence among His people. Spending any time in meditation, praise, or in worship will quickly transcend your current concerns as you begin to magnify God and experience the supernatural joy He gives. Even though the babies in our womb are unknown to us, they are well known to God. We see preborn John display joy in the presence of Mary and Jesus. Preborn babies will react to external stimuli they encounter through our actions, and this includes their joyful reaction to God's presence, as these verses claim.

Reflection: By what means do you enter God's presence? Through prayer, meditation, praise, worship, fellowshipping with the Holy Spirit? It could be any or all of the above. When you enter the presence of the Lord, realize that both you and baby are having the fullness of joy together. Be intentional about allowing your baby to enjoy the presence of the Lord.

For meditation: I knew you before I formed you in your mother's womb. Jeremiah 1:5 (NLT)

In your presence is fullness of joy. In your right hand there are pleasures forevermore. Psalm 16:11

I have chosen you and not cast you away; Don't you be afraid, for I am with you. Don't be dismayed, for I am your God. I will strengthen you. Yes, I will help you. Yes, I will uphold you with the right hand of my righteousness.   Isaiah 41:9-10

Today's word for my soul...

I'm thankful for...

Prayer focus and requests...

Casting this care upon the Lord...

Date:

Before I formed you in the womb, I knew you. Before you were born, I sanctified you.

Jeremiah 1:5

Today's word for my soul...

I'm thankful for...

Prayer focus and requests...

Casting this care upon the Lord...

Date:

Let us not be weary in doing good, for we will reap in due season, if we don't give up.

Galatians 6:9

Today's word for my soul...

I'm thankful for...

Prayer focus and requests...

Casting this care upon the Lord...

Date:

"My grace is sufficient for you, for my power is made perfect in weakness." Most gladly therefore I will rather glory in my weaknesses, that the power of Christ may rest on me.   2 Corinthians 12:9

Today's word for my soul...

I'm thankful for...

Prayer focus and requests...

Casting this care upon the Lord...

Date:

God is our refuge and strength, a very present help in trouble.

Psalm 46:1

Today's word for my soul...

_____
_____
_____
_____
_____
_____
_____
_____

I'm thankful for...

_____
_____
_____

Prayer focus and requests...

_____
_____
_____
_____
_____
_____

Casting this care upon the Lord...

_____
_____
_____

Weekly notes...

This is Week#   Date

For baby's sake, surrender.

Read the reference passage: Luke 1:26-38

Reference Verse: Mary said, "Behold, the servant of the Lord; let it be done to me according to your word." Luke 1:38

Insight

Finding out you were pregnant may have been a joyful relief of answered prayers, or a surprise blessing, that caught you off-guard. Whatever the case, the expectation of a baby usually comes with a detour, or a slowing down on your well-established path of life. This was Mary's story: she was engaged, maybe even slowly preparing for her big wedding day — complete with a delicate bridal dress, jewelry, and all that came with making her feel special. Suddenly all that changed. A Son was to be born into the world. Wedding plans would have to be placed on hold, and instead, the near future would hold plans to nest, cradle, and nurse this little One from God. Was young Mary even ready for this? Her response showed she wholeheartedly embraced it. She was fully surrendered to God's plan, allowing social and practical conveniences and even some of her own desires, to take a back seat. Part of God's perfect plan for her life was to mother this child, our Savior. God would honor her for such a brave surrender.

Reflection: Are you dealing with anything that might cause anxiety when thinking of your life after your baby is born? Are you being called to mother multiples? What are you having to put on hold? How did Mary respond to the sudden call to motherhood?

For meditation: And God is able to make all grace abound toward you, that you, always having all sufficiency in all things, may have an abundance for every good work. 2 Corinthians 9:8.

Date:

The eyes of the LORD are on the righteous, and his ears are attentive to their cry.

Psalm 34:15

Today's word for my soul...

I'm thankful for...

Prayer focus and requests...

Casting this care upon the Lord...

Date:

For everything there is a season, and a time for every purpose under heaven.

Ecclesiastes 3:1

Today's word for my soul...

I'm thankful for...

Prayer focus and requests...

Casting this care upon the Lord...

Date:

Therefore don't be anxious, saying, 'What will we eat?', 'What will we drink?' or, with 'what will we be clothed?' ... your heavenly Father knows that you need all these things. But seek first God's Kingdom, and his righteousness; and all these things will be given to you as well. Matthew 6:31-33

Today's word for my soul...

I'm thankful for...

Prayer focus and requests...

Casting this care upon the Lord...

Date:

Not that I have ... arrived at my goal, but I press on to take hold of that for which Christ Jesus took hold of me.

Philippians 3:12 (NIV)

Today's word for my soul...

I'm thankful for...

Prayer focus and requests...

Casting this care upon the Lord...

He gives the childless woman a household, making her the joyful mother of children. Hallelujah!

Psalm 113: 9 (HCSB)

Today's word for my soul...

I'm thankful for...

Prayer focus and requests...

Casting this care upon the Lord...

Weekly notes...

This is Week #   Date
_____
_____
_____
_____
_____
_____
_____
_____
_____

Magnify the Lord

Read the reference passage: Luke 1:48-55

Reference Verses: For he who is mighty has done great things for me. Holy is his name. His mercy is for generations of generations on those who fear him. (Luke 1:48-55)

Insight

This beautiful, spirit-filled song flowed out of the mouth of Mary in response to her cousin Elizabeth's praise of her presence. Rather than Mary reveling in self-glorification that she was pregnant with the Son of God, she turned her heart towards the God who chose her and favored her for this special calling: to birth the son of God in human flesh. We live in a world that increasingly tempts us to take the praise for ourselves, to glory in our self-effort. Mary helps us to turn our heart towards God. Magnifying Him that he favored us to carry and birth a child, for His purpose. We are not our own. Both mother and baby are God's workmanship created in Christ Jesus for the good works God had destined for us before we were even formed. By listening to Mary magnify the Lord, we are able to learn more about the faithfulness of God and strengthen our own faith in God.

Reflection: Meditate on the way Mary magnified the Lord after such beautiful compliments from her cousin, Elizabeth. Maybe you're receiving compliments also. Comments like, "Look at how strong you are!" or, "You're doing so well!" Whatever the compliments, it provides you with the opportunity to magnify God for His goodness to you. By doing so, you may just be strengthening the faith of your listeners too.

For meditation: O magnify the Lord with me, and let us exalt his name together. Psalm 34:3 (KJV)

Date:

(Jesus said) " Whoever receives one such little child in my name receives me."

Matthew 18:5

Today's word for my soul...

I'm thankful for...

Prayer focus and requests...

Casting this care upon the Lord...

Date:

For you formed my inmost being. You knit me together in my mother's womb. I will give thanks to you, for I am fearfully and wonderfully made.

Psalm 139:13-14

Today's word for my soul...

I'm thankful for...

Prayer focus and requests...

Casting this care upon the Lord...

Date:

And blessed is she who believed that there would be a fulfillment of what had been spoken to her by the Lord.

Luke 1:45 (NASB)

Today's word for my soul...

I'm thankful for...

Prayer focus and requests...

Casting this care upon the Lord...

Date:

(God) will take great delight in you; in his love he will ...
rejoice over you with singing.

Zephaniah 3:17 (NIV)

Today's word for my soul...

I'm thankful for...

Prayer focus and requests...

Casting this care upon the Lord...

Date:

...Be strong in the Lord, and in the strength of his might. 11 Put on the whole armor of God, that you may be able to stand against the wiles of the devil.
Ephesians 6:10-11

Today's word for my soul...

I'm thankful for...

Prayer focus and requests...

Casting this care upon the Lord...

Weekly notes...

This is Week #   Date

_____

_____

_____

_____

_____

_____

_____

_____

_____

_____

A heart of thanksgiving

Read the reference passage: 1 Samuel 2:1-10 (Hannah's Song)

Reference verse: There is no one holy like the Lord; there is no one besides you; there is no Rock like our God. 1 Samuel 1:2 (NIV)

Insight

It is such a beautiful thing to see how women exalted and worshipped the Lord through song. Hannah made a journey to Shiloh (the place of worship) after her son was born. She not only presented her son to the Lord in keeping with her vow, but she also worshipped with a song of thanksgiving that exalted the Lord for all His goodness to her. Jesus once healed ten lepers, but only one returned to give God thanks. Jesus asked for the other nine and why they had not returned to also give glory to God for the good the Lord had done for them (Luke 17:15-18). If the giving of thanks were not important, Jesus would not have mentioned it. Through it, we learn a lesson that we must remember to give God thanks for anything He does for us. Hannah has provided an excellent example for every mother to follow.

Reflection: Hannah's song of thanksgiving included her life's experience and how the Lord had intervened on her behalf. How has the Lord come through for you? Can you tell a story as Hannah told hers? Maybe not as dramatic, or perhaps even more dramatic. Punctuate your story with words of praise and thanks with specific things the Lord has done for you along this journey and season of your life.

For meditation: I will praise you, Lord, with all my heart; I will tell of all the marvelous things you have done. Psalm 9:1

Train up a child in the way he should go, and when he is old he will not depart from it.

Proverbs 22:6

Today's word for my soul...

I'm thankful for...

Prayer focus and requests...

Casting this care upon the Lord...

Date:

He took them in his arms, and blessed them, laying his hands on them.

Mark 10:16

Today's word for my soul...

I'm thankful for...

Prayer focus and requests...

Casting this care upon the Lord...

Date:

This is the boldness which we have toward him, that,
if we ask anything according to his will, he listens to us.

1 John 5:14

Today's word for my soul...

_____
_____
_____
_____
_____
_____
_____
_____
_____

I'm thankful for...

_____
_____
_____
_____

Prayer focus and requests...

_____
_____
_____
_____
_____
_____

Casting this care upon the Lord...

_____
_____
_____

Date:

The Lord is my shepherd; I have all that I need.
He lets me rest in green meadows; he leads me
beside peaceful streams. He renews my strength.

Psalm 23:1-3 (NLT)

Today's word for my soul...

I'm thankful for...

Prayer focus and requests...

Casting this care upon the Lord...

Cast your burden on the Lord, and He will sustain you;
He will never allow the righteous to be shaken.

Psalm 55:22

Today's word for my soul...

I'm thankful for...

Prayer focus and requests...

Casting this care upon the Lord...

Weekly notes...

This is Week #   Date
_____
_____
_____
_____
_____
_____
_____
_____
_____

Passing on the good news

Read the reference passage: Genesis 18:17-19

Reference verse: For I have chosen Abraham so that he will direct his children...to keep the way of the Lord by doing what is right and in so doing, the promises the Lord made to him will come to pass. (Genesis 18:19 paraphrased)

Insight

Good news awaits your little one upon arrival into this world, and you've been commissioned, by God, to deliver that news. It was always God's primary plan to use parents to deliver the truth of who He is to the next generation. Not only does God give us the assignment, but He equips us and blesses us for carrying it out, as he had assured Abraham he would: "Then I will do for Abraham all that I have promised." (Genesis 18:19). The gospel is our good news. Jesus, God's only son, came into the world to save sinners. It is captured in Jesus' very own words: "For God so loved the world, that He gave His one and only Son, that whoever believes in Him should not perish, but have eternal life." (John 3:16).

Reflection: How will you fulfill that sacred mission entrusted to you? Telling your child about Jesus may begin by just sharing the enthralling story about the birth of Jesus...and sure, it's hard to find a child who is not in awe of the true story of Christmas, but it should not end there. Move on to Jesus' real mission and continue the story to include our desperate sinful state and our need for a Messiah. Think of the ways you will introduce your child to Jesus: bedtime stories, Sunday school, teachable moments, art, songs...Trust the Lord to open your child's heart to embrace Jesus as Savior and Lord.

For meditation: Teach them to your children. Talk about them when you are at home and when you are on the road, when you are going to bed and when you are getting up. Deuteronomy 11:19 NLT

Date:

See that you don't despise one of these little ones, for I tell
you that in heaven their angels always see the face of my
Father who is in heaven.

Matthew 18:10

Today's word for my soul...

I'm thankful for...

Prayer focus and requests...

Casting this care upon the Lord...

Date:

Every good gift and every perfect gift is from above, coming down from the Father of lights, with whom can be no variation, nor turning shadow.

James 1:17

Today's word for my soul...

_____
_____
_____
_____
_____
_____
_____
_____

I'm thankful for...

_____
_____
_____
_____

Prayer focus and requests...

_____
_____
_____
_____
_____
_____

Casting this care upon the Lord...

_____
_____
_____

Date:

Fight the good fight of faith. Take hold of the eternal life to which you were called...

1 Timothy 6:12 (NIV)

Today's word for my soul...

I'm thankful for...

Prayer focus and requests...

Casting this care upon the Lord...

Date:

Trust in the Lord with all your heart, and do not rely on your own understanding; think about Him in all your ways, and He will guide you on the right paths.

Proverbs 3:5-6 (HCSB)

Today's word for my soul...

_____
_____
_____
_____
_____
_____
_____

I'm thankful for...

_____
_____
_____
_____

Prayer focus and requests...

_____
_____
_____
_____
_____

Casting this care upon the Lord...

_____
_____
_____

Date:

Have I not commanded you? Be strong and courageous. Do not be afraid; do not be discouraged, for the LORD your God will be with you wherever you go.

Joshua 1:9 (NIV)

Today's word for my soul...

I'm thankful for...

Prayer focus and requests...

Casting this care upon the Lord...

Weekly notes...

Expected Due Date: _____

Birth Venue: _____

Doctor/Midwife: _____

Nurse: _____

Delivery Day Support Crew:

My Baby's Security Blanket

Make a security blanket for your baby, writing a scripture promise on each line. Declare each of these truths, in prayer, over your baby. Take the time to meditate on them as you color in each heart for each scripture you write.

www.journalsbycatherine.com